AROUND AYLESBURY

R O B E R T   C O O K

ALAN SUTTON PUBLISHING LIMITED

Alan Sutton Publishing Limited
Phoenix Mill · Far Thrupp · Stroud
Gloucestershire · GL5 2BU

First published 1995

Copyright © Robert Cook, 1995

Cover photographs: (front) Walton Cycle &
Motor Works, 1910; (back) a Sunday School
treat in Aylesbury Vale, 1908.

British Library Cataloguing in Publication Data.
A catalogue record for this book is available from
the British Library.

ISBN 0-7509-0838-6

Typeset in 9/10 Sabon.
Typesetting and origination by
Alan Sutton Publishing Limited.
Printed in Great Britain by
Ebenezer Baylis, Worcester.

We can see by the giant 'H' on one of these little chimneys in Pebble Lane that television
has arrived in early 1950s Aylesbury. But with only the test card to watch in those days,
Mrs Woodford would rather be out on this sunny morning, enjoying a chat through a
neighbour's window. Mrs Woodford was one of the first to join the Darby and Joan
Club, and her husband was a brickmaker at Hartwell.

Contents

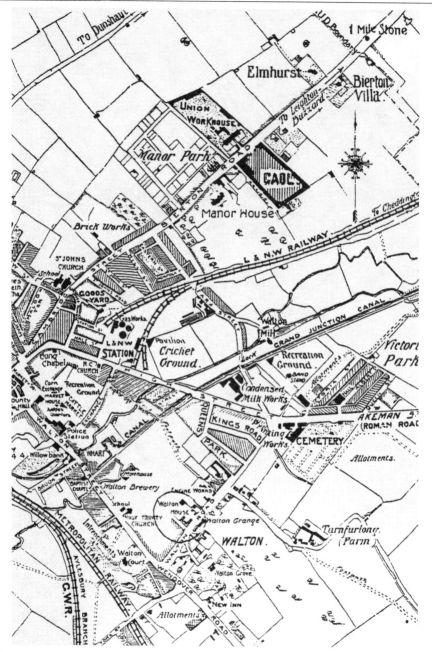

This 1907 map shows that the town was well served by railways, a canal and ancient roads. Industry was still mainly linked to agriculture, but the printing industry was well established. By 1910 Bifurcated Tubular Rivets had arrived and was building Iris motor cars.

Introduction

Once upon a time, living among the first plants, there were dinosaurs in the land we now call Aylesbury Vale. These lumbering creatures could never have imagined what their lives would precede. Those were momentous times in 'Jurassic Park', long before recorded history. The first birds appeared; Oxford and Kimmeridge Clays and Portland Stone were laid down. For a long time there were no people, and nature ruled.

So where did Aylesbury begin? Basically with the weather. Rain made the rivers which became the Thame and its tributaries. These shaped and drained an area which we call the Vale, with pleasant hills rising on either side. It is fertile and rich with a clay soil, suitable for brick making.

In the age of ancient Britons there was no trace of what we now call Aylesbury. The Romans came and carved out Akeman Street (now the A41). Their Saxon mercenaries seem to have left their mark at Walton, where they would have been living while guarding the Roman road. But apart from that, there is little sign of Roman impact on the two rounded outcrops of Portland Stone which eventually became Aylesbury and Walton (though the former finally engulfed the latter). The Celtic Britons had these sites much to themselves until Cuthwulf's Anglo-Saxon army forced them out. The place name probably derives from 'Aigle's Burgh' (town).

Anglo-Saxons brought the three-field farming system, with ridge and furrow drainage – pushing back the boundaries of native Chiltern woodland. Though they did not inflict a reign of terror (provided later by invading Normans), King Offa of Mercia kept order, reinforced by Christianity – an even more powerful controlling force once the Normans had created St Mary's Church and a Franciscan friary.

The Danes became a serious nuisance in 921 and the Saxons retaliated under Edward the Confessor. But there was no real stability until William the Conqueror brought Norman feudalism in 1066.

And so, thereafter, Aylesbury took shape. The lordship became a key to local control and was on sale to a chosen few. Through marriage it passed to Sir William Boleyn, father of Anne, in 1515. The arable lands were divided into strips within the open fields and let out to tenants, who worked as virtual slaves.

The open-field system lasted without problem until plague struck in the fourteenth century. As Buckinghamshire is a thoroughfare county and Aylesbury a route junction, a lot of grain passed through, and rats, travelling with it, carried the plague bacillus. The resulting high death rate created a labour shortage, forcing more land into enclosed pasture. The Industrial Revolution accelerated this enclosure into compact farms because there was need for more efficient farming to feed the growing cities.

In the meantime Aylesbury had received borough status in 1554 as reward for supporting Mary Tudor's accession. The town received rights to burgesses, aldermen, fairs, a weekly market and two shire knights (MPs). The stage was set for locals to enjoy the curious pleasures of cock fighting and cock throwing!

Political corruption was rife until the late nineteenth century. In 1872 the secret ballot reduced intimidation by landowners and employers. By 1888 all men, regardless of wealth, could vote. Two world wars brought contact with the wider world and helped to change the role of women. But life remained hard for most people. Judy Ounsworth remembers walking 3 miles to get coal, which was still on ration in 1947: 'We used to push an old trolley made from old pram wheels to collect our coal, which cost half a crown. We had to queue up and hope they didn't run out before it was our turn. The coal was not house coal but steam coal, which we burnt on an open fire mixed with coal dust or wood and even old vegetable peelings. My mum used to send me and my two brothers so that we could all get in the queue, outside the old gas works. Sometimes if we were lucky we all got some.'

But the age of plenty and an everlasting feast was just around the corner. Since 1945 Aylesbury has shared in the London overspill and Commonwealth immigration, traffic congestion, rising crime, improved health care, two major redevelopments and industrial estates. As the county town since the reign of Henry VIII, its population has risen from 3,447 in 1811 to nearly 60,000 in 1995. With all these changes and rapid growth, Aylesbury is bound to have an identity problem, worsened by doubts over the county's future. But it has never lacked curiosities.

Robert Cook, March 1995

Kingsbury, summer 1962. This was once a busy bus station, especially on market days, connecting local villages and towns with Aylesbury.

ON THE STREETS
WHERE THEY
LIVED

'What is this life if, full of care,

We have no time to stand and stare?'

Market Square, 1926.

THE CORN FIELDS, CALIFORNIA

CALIFORNIA, AYL...

THE BRIDGE, CALIFORNIA

California, Aylesbury.

THE MILL STREAM

These five tranquil scenes of California, Aylesbury, are a far cry from their US namesake and indeed from California, Aylesbury, today. The railway footbridge is the only recognisable landmark. Schwarzkopf's factory now dominates the landscape on the bridge's southern side. The area to the north experienced substantial redevelopment in the 1990s; a former garden, which had become a car-park and Friarage Road in the 1960s, became a Safeway supermarket and car-park. On the far side of Friarage Road, Friar's Square experienced a face-lift. When the new square was opened, the *Bucks Herald* reported: 'The good news about Friar's Square 1993 is that it replaces the former edifice of the same name and that it has an attractive colour scheme of cream and green. But that is about it.'

The parish of Walton was soon absorbed by the fast-growing Aylesbury town. The houses shown here are mainly Regency; Holy Trinity Church is just visible on the right, *c.* 1890.

Tring Road in the late nineteenth century. This route followed the line of the Roman Akeman Street and joined with New Road in 1826. New Road became High Street, making it easier to enter the town and soon attracting a variety of shopkeepers.

Buckingham Street, late nineteenth century. This had become part of the turnpike road to Buckingham in 1721.

Before the motor bus, folk came from the villages by carrier's cart on market day. Carriers parked in the yards of the various inns. Buses needed much more space and Kingsbury Square, shown here, was the established depot by 1929.

The round-house, at the junction of Cambridge Street and High Street, is one of the town's oldest surviving landmarks. Kingsbury and Market Square also meet here, keeping policemen very busy at the time of this photograph. The traffic-lights arrived in 1934. Special Constable Ron Rayner remembers directing traffic at this spot for up to two hours at a time.

This closer view of High Street shows that traders were well established by 1920, but there was still a residential element. Notice also that the motor car is beginning to make its presence felt.

Kingsbury, mid-1930s. The son of a London horse-bus driver, Edward M. Cain was the driving force behind the Red Rover Omnibus Company. With his brothers, he chose Aylesbury as the destination for an express coach route because he had an aunt living there. Roads were improving, especially after county councils took over highway maintenance in 1931, and pneumatic tyres made buses a worthy rival to the railways. All this was a far cry from the 1820s, when eight stage-coach services ran from Aylesbury; the *Aylesbury News* advised stage-coach travellers that 'to attain maximum comfort . . . they should drink a good tankard of cold ale and rub their hands and faces in snow before the start'. Stage-coaches were usurped by the Aylesbury–Cheddington Railway, which reduced travelling time to London from 6 hours to 95 minutes in 1839. But the 1930s was the age of motor vehicles. London Transport was created to unify transport in and around the capital, forcing Edward Cain towards services for the local area. His daughter Olive remembers living over their offices in Kingsbury in the late 1920s, next door to the Victoria Club: 'He was very particular about time-keeping, out at 8 a.m. to see the buses off. They were garaged in Park Street. Dinner bang on 12. Back for tea at 4. Then out again at 5 p.m. into Kingsbury. He stood by the Victoria Club to see the last bus off just after 9 p.m., then went into the Victoria Club for a drink. If there was an accident he was always on the spot. He was a working managing director.'

Church Street, late 1930s. Nowadays it is difficult to find a parking space here. Early this century Dr Baker used the house on the right as his living quarters, surgery and drug dispensary. He followed a tradition started by the previous resident and eminent local doctor, Robert Ceely, a driving force behind the establishment of the Royal Bucks Hospital. Ceely also won admiration for fighting the cholera epidemic of 1832. Dr Baker is remembered for having the first motor car in Aylesbury. His old residence is now a store of memories as the home of the county museum.

Primrose and Rose Woodford outside their Mount Street home, just before the First World War. Mrs Woodford took the vicar's advice, as he passed by her open front door, and named her new baby after the day, which was Primrose Day. The old parish workhouse was near here and 'Ducky' Weston carried on breeding ducks in Mount Street until 1956. 'All right, my duck' has become a local catchphrase.

Aylesbury's much needed inner relief road between Exchange Street and New Street was approved in June 1983. This picture shows the junction of New Street and Cambridge Street in July 1947. The poster on the wall behind the two girls is advertising the Granada Cinema; the film showing was *Dual Alibi* with Herbert Lom. The cinema closed to become a bingo hall in October 1972.

'Singing Dustman' John Otway's birthplace, 17 Whitehall Street, 1951. John's grandmother and sister pose. John's mother, Pat Otway, recalls: 'When two buses passed they came right up on the pavement and you could shake hands with the passengers through our bedroom window. They were gorgeous cottages; a tiny circular staircase led up to the attic.' The cottages were pulled down for road widening in 1958.

The Otways moved to this end terrace, 35 Wendover Road. Four years later road improvements caught up with them and all three properties were demolished to make way for the famous gyratory system, which created an island of properties at the junction of Wendover and Stoke roads. Ex-shepherd Jack Otway was obviously finding Aylesbury more uplifting than his native Lake District!

The peacefulness suggested by this view of the round-house in the late forties contrasts with the scene on page 11, but was to be short lived. Traffic-lights have arrived and soon so would a multitude of newcomers. By this time council house building was going full speed and industrial estates were planned for the periphery. The old town centre so far was intact. But a new kind of town dweller was on the way, with much higher expectations than older natives. Sometimes there was conflict. In 1964 Carlton Close, on the western tip of the Bicester Road estate, had problems with children playing at night and at weekends: they were causing rows and waking babies. Resident Stan Clarke told the *Bucks Herald*: 'A proper recreation ground for the children, with adequate amenities and supervision, is needed. The council refuse tip in Meadowcroft, where children sometimes play, is a deathtrap.' G.B. Hannay, Borough Surveyor, said there was a strip of land left specially for children's play space. Oddly, this was the site of the proposed northern bypass and there seemed to be a certain amount of planning confusion!

A WORLD OF
THEIR OWN

Down by the riverside, Hartwell Estate, 1907.

This was the Aylesbury–Buckingham road at Shipton just before the First World War. The London–Holyhead telegraph poles on the right must have seemed as ugly as today's satellite dishes. But there was no standing in the way of mass communication. At least in those days you could safely stand in the middle of the road. The First World War advanced the motor vehicle and changed the picture. This scene is at the bottom of a long hill south of Winslow. The road curving to the left in the distance passes over a humpback bridge. This was the scene of numerous accidents, such as the one involving the daily LCS milk tanker, shown on page 81. Aylesbury was the home of Bucks County Council, which took control of highway maintenance in 1931. Its first step forward was to produce a structure plan for the whole county, detailing road improvements to accommodate an expected massive increase in motor-vehicle usage. The plan spelt death to many byways, while offering to ease pressure on others such as this one, preserved since the late thirties as a lay-by and picnic area. But with 11,000 hectares of countryside being consumed for residential development every year, Bucks is a prime target for developers. There have been protests against threats to beauty spots like the Wendover green belt and historic Dinton Manor. Property developer Russell Smith, owner of sixteenth-century Dinton Hall and the later mock castle, criticised opponents of his hotel and leisure scheme as people who 'live in a world of their own'.

Dunsham Lane just before the development of Elmhurst Estate in 1962. This lane ran from near the old ambulance station in Buckingham Road to Dunsham Farm.

Dr John Lee of Hartwell House was an Egyptologist, lawyer, politician, gentleman, teetotaller and astronomer. This view of architect Joseph Bonomi II's Egyptian structure by the lane to Lower Hartwell is testament to Lee's enthusiasm for a more ancient civilisation. In the nineteenth century Hartwell House was also equipped with an observatory. The photograph dates from the 1890s.

A farmhouse on the Hartwell Estate, late 1890s. Hartwell House (see page 85) was probably enlarged from an earlier house inherited by Sir Alexander Hampden in 1570, passing through marriage to the Lees of East Claydon and Morton. In 1690 Sir Thomas laid out an elaborate formal garden. The house was later home to the exiled Louis XVIII.

Granborough, 8 miles north of Aylesbury, was part of Winslow Manor. Carriers' carts, trains and then buses pulled it increasingly into Aylesbury's orbit. In 1907 it was still fairly self-sufficient.

Enclosure of Granborough parish's big fields left few grass verges as wide as this one. What a wonderful sight these youngsters make, their spirits no doubt lifted by the visit from the Bucks Gospel Car, *c.* 1907.

Granborough Girl Guides, *c.* 1910. One can imagine them chanting the local skipping rhyme: 'I am a Girl Guide dressed in blue, / These are the actions I have to do, / Salute to the King, bow to the Queen, / And turn my back on the girl in green.'

Granborough Road station, 9½ miles from Aylesbury, pictured in the late 1920s. This line connected Aylesbury with Verney Junction and relied very much on the support and motive power of the GWR, which also ran into Aylesbury via Princes Risborough. The Aylesbury–Buckingham railway was inspired by the Duke of Buckingham. Popular with livestock transporters, it closed to passengers in 1936.

North Marston, viewed from St Mary's Church, mid-1920s. Sir John Schorne, its vicar from 1290 to 1314, blessed the village well. Therefore, it was said, the water gained great healing power. From 1314 until Sir John's bones were removed to Windsor in 1478, pilgrims came from miles around to drink the water.

The Firs, 1921. This was one of seven de Rothschild mansions within 8 miles of Aylesbury and made the village of Whitchurch famous by earning the nickname 'Churchill's toyshop' during the Second World War. A number of ingenious weapons were made there – not without accident. Post-war uses included research into steel by manufacturers Richard Thomas and Baldwin, and shell rocket propulsion.

Waddesdon is about 5 miles west of Aylesbury on the Roman Akeman Street. Baron Ferdinand de Rothschild bought the manorial estate in 1874 and had his mansion built on Lodge Hill. It follows the style of Loire Valley chateaux favoured in the nineteenth century.

The steam-mill near Waddesdon, *c.* 1898. The bearded figure in the doorway (far left) is Joseph Taylor, the miller. This was a replacement mill, built in the 1890s. It still stands but is no longer a working mill.

The ultimate in environmental friendship: a windmill near Waddesdon. Milling gradually became larger scale and by the thirties Hills and Partridge's Mill in Aylesbury was the major operator. However, in the last decade even that has been abandoned.

A cow takes a bath at Harry Rogers' duck farm at Meadle, 6 miles south-west of Aylesbury. The ducks look on as if in amazement. Ealing coalman Harry bought the smallholding for £675 in 1923. Mr East used to collect the ducks from a cluster of duck farms in the area and take them to the station on his Dunelt motor bike and side-car in the late twenties.

This is Harry Rogers' wife Alice and daughter Ivy enjoying all the benefits of country air on the duck farm in 1929. Harry's son Len (see page 28) won a scholarship to High Wycombe Technical School, but the cost of travelling made it more sensible to choose a life of farming, working initially with his father, rather than take a job in the big town.

Aston Clinton is sheltered by the rising Chiltern Hills, about 4 miles east of Aylesbury. The early Aston Martin cars were tested on the slopes of Aston Hill and so earned their name. Long before that, in 1887, this school had been built, educating boys in the three Rs and keeping them away from the distractions of the opposite sex. Girls were educated by the de Rothschild family at a straw-plaiting school.

Granborough's school was more enlightened. These boys and girls of the 1920s enjoyed life together at the tiny village school.

Real horse power still had a future when this picture was taken at Wingrave Forge, *c.* 1930. The sign above the horse's head reads 'Mat Maker', which was the occupation of the blacksmith's brother-in-law George Rickard. George had been blinded in the First World War and lived with the blacksmith, Tommy Woodruffe.

Harry Rogers in the driving seat of his Calcot car at Meadle Farm, 1924. To the right is his son Len. When this car was a bit older, Len was allowed to use it to bring milk up from their other smallholding at Little Marsh, until he tipped the churns over three days running. Then his dad warned: 'You'll have to go back to the horse and cart.'

Local children pose in front of Granborough grocer Bill Newman's new 15 h.p. Ford delivery van, bought from Long's Aylesbury Motor Company. The vehicle cost £175, and with petrol priced at a mere shilling per gallon the Newmans' old horse went into retirement.

The Newmans' van retired in 1943; one day Bill was loading his van outside home, ready for the morning deliveries. He looked up to spot a silver plane glinting in the sky and as soon as he saw a cigar-shaped object falling towards him he rushed inside to rescue his wife. The couple were saved by sheltering under the inglenook fireplace. The bomb destroyed two houses and left a huge crater. When a Winslow breakdown truck came to tow the van away for repair, the crippled vehicle collapsed into a heap. The US Army Air Force was responsible for the disaster but the British government blocked compensation in case it ended up with the bill. The Newman home was the second one along the lane shown in this picture. It was behind the wheelwright's shop in the foreground. This view looks east, in the 1930s.

Seen from under the canopy of a recently refurbished Stoke Mandeville station, British Railways' Standard class 5 locomotive no. 73010 passes the colourful garden with a Nottingham-bound train, 29 July 1965. Aylesbury Town was minutes away, but its main-line days were nearly over – ending on 3 September 1966.

Dinton Green, a few miles west of Aylesbury, late 1940s. Dinton is famed for being the site of Bigg's Cave. John Bigg was allegedly Charles I's executioner and his resulting madness was supposed to have driven him to become a recluse.

Sidney Dickins of Hanover Farm, Addington, competing in the county show at Hartwell Park with his favourite chestnut, Robin, in 1948.

Young Jeremy Sellars takes Hookey over the jumps at the same show.

POWER TO THE PEOPLE

Walking under Old Beams restaurant,

early 1960s.

The mayor's coach and procession pass a block comprising the old army drill hall, George Hotel and Bodega (Seaton's wine merchants), 1890s. McIlroy's the draper's is just visible on the left. This was formerly Polden and Gurney's, to which ladies used to be delivered by carriage. But the world was changing fast. Aylesbury's *Bucks Herald* first reported local news in 1792 (the present *Herald* began in 1832) and the popular nationals reported a broader background. All were helping to shape the minds and expectations of increasingly literate local people. Tory Prime Minister Benjamin Disraeli lived nearby at Hughenden Manor from 1847 until his death in 1881. He accompanied his beloved Queen Victoria on a visit to Aylesbury. It was he who first extended votes to working-class men in 1867, and his colleague Robert Lowe is supposed to have said: 'We must now educate our masters', thus encouraging the 1870 State Education Act. Aylesbury's corporate status had been granted in 1554 as a reward for supporting Mary Tudor's accession, but power remained with the rich. John Wilkes may have cried freedom in his bid to become Aylesbury MP but he knew he had to pay for it. He wrote to his friend Dell in 1757. 'I will give two guineas per man, with the promise of whatever more offers.' Success cost him £7,000, proving perhaps that freedom is no more than the recognition of necessity. The 1950s made other offers, namely socialism and consumerism. The former was never popular, but the latter was embraced wholeheartedly. After many town-centre changes, Aylesbury contemplates more, in its efforts to rival the north Bucks mecca of Milton Keynes. Perhaps local songster John Otway sums it all up best with his immortal lyric: 'Cor baby, that's really free.'

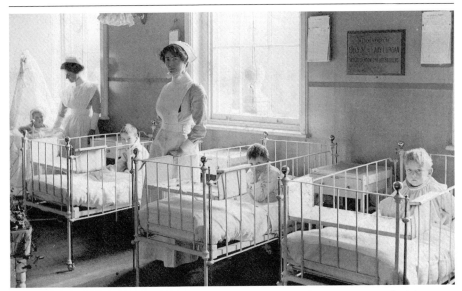

Royal Bucks Hospital (Bucks Infirmary), children's ward, 1914. Parental visits were discouraged because they unsettled the patients. Florence Nightingale virtually designed the building. She was ahead of her time and, as sister-in-law to Sir Harry Verney, was well placed to make things happen. The hospital foundation stone was laid by Lady Verney on 30 April 1861. John Lee LL D of Hartwell opened it the following year.

Simon Vincent Robinson, founder of Robinson's removal firm, with wife Alice Ellen and daughters Peggy and Joan. Mr Robinson came from Cheadle, Staffordshire, to work for two uncles by the name of Bloor. Their business was in Market Square. The business was failing, but a client gave Mr Robinson £100 to start up on his own.

A statue commemorating Prime Minister Benjamin Disraeli stands at the junction of Market Square and High Street. The London Joint Stock Bank (right) is now the Midland. The sixteenth-century timbered Crown Hotel (left) was complete with bowling green and stable yard. All was demolished in 1937.

Education was hardly styled for 'masters' (see page 34) when this picture of St Mary's schoolchildren was taken in 1910. Primrose Woodford is fifth from the left in the second row. 'Ducky' Weston's son is in the front row, far left. Schoolmistress Morris is on the right. Aylesbury's youngsters learned the basics at this elementary school and then chose from an increasing variety of local job opportunities. Girls may have had less adventurous choices, such as domestic service, silk weaving, lace making or the local basket works (using local osier beds), but at least they could not be called up for the 'Great War', which was not far away.

Three old characters labouring in the fields around Granborough early this century. The countryside was a haven for hunting, shooting, ferreting and poaching.

'Pigeon' Green, a celebrated Aylesbury character and odd-job man born in Wendover to George and Charlotte Tomlin, who had married on 7 November 1858. He was famous for his daily buttonhole. His age was given as 92 in November 1951.

Farm labouring was still a major
occupation when this picture was taken in
Granborough in about 1897.

Rose Woodford's wedding picture, taken in Park Street in the 1920s. Rose is seated and her
sister Primrose is to her right. The Miller sisters, Primrose's sisters-in-law, are on Rose's left.
Primrose says her name suits her because she has been prim and proper all her life.

A proud Sergeant James Harford Blackmore, *c.* 1905. He died on 1 April 1915 in a humble Aylesbury cottage after a military career which included the Crimean War and Indian Mutiny. The local vicar, Revd C.W. Pearson, saved him from the ignominy of a pauper's grave, giving him a military funeral. The firing party was furnished by the East Yorkshires, with four bearers from the Northumberland Fusiliers, both regiments being quartered in the neighbourhood. James was 18 when he enlisted in 1841. It was understood that he was one of the party concerned in rounding up the notorious bushrangers, Ned Kelly and his gang, who were rampant in New South Wales between 1870 and 1878. The French awarded James the Médaille Militaire of the French Empire during the Crimean War.

Simon Vincent Robinson worked hard to build up his furniture and removal business early this century. As a Freemason he found time to look after the needs of the less fortunate. He is seen here in the late 1950s. His masonic lodge was Aylesbury No. 4534. The Masons originated as a craft society.

This photograph shows the Duke of York (later George VI) opening four new houses in York Place on 2 July 1928. Presented to him were Councillor Walter Jowett (chairman of the Housing Trust Committee), W.H. Taylor (architect) and F.R. Cannon of Webster and Cannon Builders.

Two ladies enjoy a morning chat over the fence in Park Street, *c.* 1935.

Kathleen and Hilda Whitlock (centre and right) with friend. They were pupils at Aylesbury Grammar School between the wars, when the system was still co-educational.

The Brazier brothers, veteran cattle dealers from Granborough, shortly after the Second World War. Fred 'Uncle Ted' Brazier is seated while Charlie leans on the railings during bidding in the Aylesbury ring.

Sally Girvan. She was Carnival Queen at the town carnival, which raised money for the Royal Bucks Hospital extension fund in July 1935. Journalist John How noted: 'It was so hot, even the borough mace-bearer switched hands to lick his two penny ice-cream during the carnival parade.'

A boy and his 'grampy' in front of Queen's Park School, early 1950s. Dick Goodchild recalled: 'Queen's Park was commandeered for a hospital during World War One and we were pushed around the town to do our schooling in any old hut.'

Dick Goodchild (left) with Bifurcated Tubular Rivets (the 'Biffs') colleague Harry Fincher, getting Harry's best onions ready for a 1950s flower show. It was a tradition around Aylesbury for men to do their bit growing vegetables on the allotments. Dick spent most of his working life at the 'Biffs' – though he expected an early dismissal when, as a boy pulling his gangrenous boss on a trolley around the works, he tipped him over.

Rose Goodchild (née Woodford), one of the first Park Street residents to join the 1950s media revolution and buy a television.

Nurses Ann Hughes (left) and Mary Keily just back from Sunday morning church, standing outside Tindal nurses' home, *c.* 1960. Ann was recruited via Dublin and her father told her that if she did not like nursing in Aylesbury she should ring Mr Kilduff at the post office and he would send her the fare home to Ireland.

Ann stayed and enjoyed the hard work and hectic social life with her cosmopolitan colleagues, pictured here in about 1960. They enjoyed playing hurley in the nurses' home corridors and tying door knobs together with their stockings.

Enoch Powell took exception to the number of Commonwealth immigrants and is seen here addressing Conservative women at the Borough Assembly Hall in March 1965. Sir Spencer Summers attended as Conservative MP for Aylesbury. Starting with European Voluntary Workers after the war, the town has continued to develop as a multi-cultural society. There are about 2,800 Pakistanis in Aylesbury. Most originate from the Mirpur District of Azad Kashmir.

Tindal nurses relax outside the canteen hut, 1959. The temporary huts were still going strong when the General Hospital closed down in the 1970s. The hospital was named after the Tindal family, who owned the manor and were involved with building the Union Workhouse, which had occupied this site.

Part of the workhouse building is shown here, after it had become Tindal Hospital. 'We wear short shorts' was a popular 1950s song by the Vernon Girls, and seen here playing tennis in 1959, nurse Ann Hughes could easily have been mistaken for one of them!

Nurses entertain patients at Tindal Hospital Christmas party, 1959. Ann Hughes (left) and Dawn Siever sing. Dawn was a good friend of the popular Cockatoos band and persuaded them to provide backing music.

Nurse Renée Stone graduates from Tindal nursing training in 1961 and receives a prize. She went on to nurse in Malaya.

''Ello, 'ello, 'ello, what's all this then?' In June 1964 a 15 ft deep hole appeared in Aylesbury High Street and here we see borough surveyor G.B. Hannay and a constable investigating. The cause was a burst water main washing away the ground below.

The Kimber family arrived in Aylesbury as part of the 1960s' Greater London Scheme. The town was developing a range of new industries on Gatehouse Estate. For the Kimbers, life on Oakfield Estate was a lot better than the eight years they had spent living in one room in the heart of north London. Mrs Kimber could not understand why some of her neighbours moved back to London after only a few months.

Christine Hall, Miss Aylesbury Jubilee 1966, contrasts with her 1935 'sister' (see page 44), but she's still uplifting! With sadness the *Bucks Advertiser* commented in April 1964: 'Every day a little glamour and individuality is lost as we all conform to an average pattern. Eccentrics are becoming more and more rare. We solemnly fill in forms, pigeon hole ourselves apparently quite happily and try to be generally like everyone else.' Not so Christine!

John Otway with his 1970s' punk rock partner 'Wild Willy Barrett'. Becoming a dustman was part of his strategy to become a star. His big chance came with a group auditioning for *Opportunity Knocks*. His biography records: 'Throughout the performance he rocked and rolled and looked delighted at his first proper gig. Shortly afterwards someone explained to him that the group had unplugged his guitar at the start of the song and were more than a little amused at his enthusiastic playing. The hurt was compounded when, speaking to his mother about his wish to get a band, he was told: 'John, why do you always want to do what the other kids are doing?' Aylesbury really got serious about pop music when kilted pop singer Jacky Dennis opened the Record Centre in Kingsbury in the 1950s. Since then it has spawned Marillion and their hit 'Kayleigh', with the very local image of 'Do you remember, cherry blossom in the market square.' David Bowie, Genesis, Roxy Music, Blondie and the Ramones are just a few of the big names who have played Aylesbury venues. The Rolling Stones struggled through winter fog in 1964 to play at the Granada. They were later called to an Aylesbury Court drugs trial. David Stops, Friars Music Club founder, recalled Aylesbury's Borough Assembly Hall venue in 1977 as: 'A fantastic venue. It had terrible acoustics but it had an incredible vibe about it and a lot of people remember it as the golden period of Friars. Our success was in booking bands just before they made it big.' The Borough Assembly Hall was formerly known as the Market Theatre, and was once the home to the Manchester Rep. Ronnie Barker started his acting career there.

Bert Hughes with his collection of scale-model locomotives from the Great Central Railway, early 1970s. The GCR ran through Stoke Mandeville using the Metropolitan Line as far as Aylesbury and then from 1899 carried on to Sheffield and Manchester. In its final days the service only went as far as Nottingham. This service ended in 1966. Bert received *The Wonder Book of Railways* as a Christmas present in 1919, thus beginning a life-time interest. Regular holidays with relatives in Stoke Mandeville led to permanent employment in the district and the opportunity for closer study of the GCR. During quiet moments in the army he began his model making. After the war he returned to work at Calvert Fletton brickworks near Aylesbury and enjoyed regular train rides to Calvert. Gradually he made accurate models of all the main GCR locomotives; they have been used in promotional displays by British Rail.

John Hampden's statue was unveiled on 27 June 1912. Hampden was killed at Chalgrove Field in a Civil War against undemocratic expenditure. In 1988, to accommodate redevelopment, the statue was moved 15 yd at a cost of £10,000. Now, instead of pointing a warning finger at County Hall, he points towards a travel agent's!

Section Four

DOING TIME

Making hay while the sun shines on Rogers' farm

at Meadle, 1935.

AYLESBURY RAILWAY.

FIVE POUNDS REWARD.

Some evil-disposed Person or Persons have lately *feloniously Stolen and carried away*, a quantity of RAILS, STAKES, and MATERIALS, belonging to the Company, for which any Offender, on Conviction, is liable to Transportation for Seven Years.

Several STAKES driven into the Ground for the purpose of setting out the Line of Railway, *have also been Pulled up and Removed*, by which a Penalty of Five Pounds for each Offence has been incurred, half Payable to the Informer and half to the Company.

The above Reward will be paid on Conviction, in addition to the Penalty, to any Person who will give Evidence sufficient to Convict any Offender guilty of either of the above Crimes, on application to Mr. HATTEN or Mr. ACTON TINDAL, of Aylesbury.

By Order of the Directors.

Aylesbury, August 18th, 1838.

May, Printer, Aylesbury.

This poster speaks for itself. Other local punishments once included a prison treadmill for pumping up the town's water.

The new gaol, which opened in 1845. It was more comfortable and was popular with sightseers. On 28 March 1845 a crowd of 10,000 flocked in from surrounding villages to watch John Tawell hang, for the murder of Sarah Hart. He was the first criminal to be caught by means of the telegraph. He had escaped by train, but the police telegraphed ahead and he was caught when he alighted. On a happier note Charlie Drake filmed *The Cracksman* here in May 1964.

Aylesbury High Street station, *c.* 1950. North and Randall Mineral Water premises are visible on the left. Both this line to Cheddington and the Euston main line opened in 1839.

A quiet scene on the Aylesbury branch of the Grand Union Canal, *c.* 1898. St Mary's Church is visible on the horizon. The branch was opened in 1814, halving the cost of coal to 1*s* 3*d* per cwt.

Arthur Harvey-Taylor was one of eleven children. Born in Waddesdon, into a flour-milling family, he bought Aylesbury coal merchant J. Landon's narrow-boat fleet in 1923. Taking coal to Nestles and the steam laundry was his staple traffic. When the power station was run by the Town Council a pair of boats was loaded daily. Here *Roger* and *Daphne* await loads at Brentford. Straw-board was also carried to Hazell's printers.

Aylesbury High Street, with trade well established and shop assistants working very long hours, c. 1897. Longleys' ample premises (with the flag pole) sold all sorts of clothes, furniture and hairdressing for both sexes.

Housing developed along Bicester Road in the nineteenth century, and was quickly followed by a range of industries, including Cubitt's car making. The gallows were originally along this route, by the junction with Griffin Lane. Drovers were once a regular sight en route to market, and trotting ponies were bred in adjacent fields.

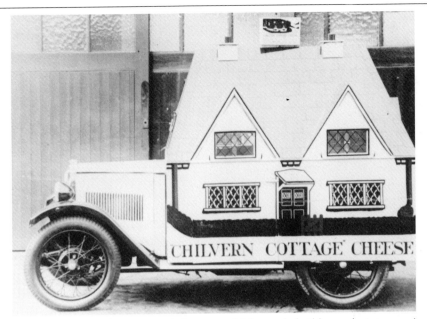

A Chilvern Cottage Cheese van of the type which coach builder and motor engineer Ron Rayner used to work on, late 1920s. They were built at Keith Garages and consisted of plywood over ash frames. They delivered the local Golden Acre butter.

KEITH
Garage

BICESTER ROAD · AYLESBURY
(Proprietors: A. MILLS & S. ADAMS)

Motor · Electrical
& General Engineers

PRIVATE CARS *for* HIRE

PETROL, OILS, AND ACCESSORIES
Phone, Aylesbury 259

Adams left this partnership to start his own business in Tring Road and Keith Garages found fame taking over the Red Rover Bus Company in 1955.

Loading magazines and bound books in 'kennels' at Hazell's, 1903. Before the lorry, cart loads were taken to Stoke Mandeville station for rail delivery to London. The cost via this station was cheaper than via Aylesbury.

Hazell and Watson printers moved from Hatton Garden to Friarage Road, Aylesbury, in 1867. They expanded rapidly after Oscar Viney joined and took these Tring Road premises. This picture shows the extension to the main block underway in 1906.

Hazell's No. 1 composing room, 1912.
Mr Woodward (wearing a hat) is facing
F.T. Flower. Horace Glover is on the far
right. Note that electric lighting is in use.

Hand trolleys and a horse-drawn cart at work in Hazell's, 1912.

Walton Cycle & Motor Works, Walton Street, 1910. Here William Stanley began assembling bicycles from Raleigh components when cycling was in its heyday. Increasing his skills, he began to make his own components and ran into patent disputes with Raleigh. During the First World War his works made shell cases. Most of this site is now taken up by a roundabout, built to cope with a more persistent type of traffic.

Simon Vincent Robinson's first shop in Silver Street, 1918. The retail side of the business moved to 59 High Street in 1924.

Robinson's removal men at work in the 1940s. The firm quickly earned a reputation for quality and reliability through hard work.

Robinson's moved to these premises in Friarage Road in 1916. This site has now been developed as Duck Farm Court and Robinson's has moved to purpose-built premises off Rabans Lane.

Simon Vincent Robinson started out with a horse and cart but the First World War stimulated the development of reliable commercial vehicles. This picture shows his first lorry, which is based on a 1910 AEC London bus chassis and was purchased in 1915 for £38. The men are, left to right, Simon Vincent Robinson, Jim Frost, Tom Alexander.

Thorpe's Garage viewed from a corner of the old Slipper Baths in Bourbon Street, late 1920s. Mr Thorpe also ran a taxi service, and Ron Rayner became garage manager soon after the Second World War.

The customised Rolls-Royce owned by Armenian millionaire Nubar Gulbenkian (see page 105), outside Thorpe's Garage, early 1950s. Ron Rayner remembers travelling to Gulbenkian's Hoggeston mansion to service this vehicle. He said: 'Because of the modifications Rolls-Royce cancelled the warranty. But nothing serious ever went wrong with it.'

Chamberlain's workshop, Buckingham Street, late 1940s. From the earliest days of motor transport the business handled anything from building car bodies to horse-boxes. It closed in the early 1980s to make way for Sainsbury's.

Kingsbury Square, late 1940s. This bus was bound for Oxford, city of dreaming spires, at a time when Aylesbury still had time to dream. Buses had conductors, easing the pressure on the driver and giving him someone to talk to before the long run back to the garage.

International Alloys' ex-RAF Queen Mary-type transporter at work in the Bicester Road area just after the Second World War. The business was founded by Mr Jakobi at a time when the war had left a lot of scrap metal lying about. Local haulage company ACH eventually took on a lot of carrying for International Alloys. The company base made way for a new Tesco superstore in the early 1980s.

One of Aylesbury's VSG banana vans parked outside Waddesdon Manor gates, 1954. Judy Ounsworth remembers her delight when passing VSG's gates with her mum just after the war and seeing bananas again – 'loads of them!'

This works bus, photographed in about 1958, carried staff to Airtech Ltd, 4 miles south of Aylesbury at Haddenham's old wartime airfield. Airtech converted surplus war planes for passenger services, which were booming in the late 1940s. Aylesbury continued its link with aircraft technology when Airtrainers moved in to make aircraft simulators. The firm later merged with its competitor, Redifon.

A United Counties bus passes two advertisements for Page's, the local bakers, 1950s. Irene Mortimer remembers being the first conductress working for United Counties' predecessors, Eastern National: 'There was a better service. The earliest morning route was the early workmen's at 5.30 a.m. from Southcourt to International Alloys.'

Ron Rayner left Thorpe's garage to start his own business in Stocklake in the late 1940s. He was helped by his wife, a young Irish nurse whom he had met when he was the volunteer St John's ambulance driver who drove her from the station to the nurses' home on the day she arrived. Ron stands here with assistant Bill Brooks after winning the All England American Heavy Wreckers Challenge trophy for the third time, in the 1970s. The contest was for drivers of pre-1950 American trucks.

The *Bucks Herald* was established in 1792 by Mr McDonald, who married the widow of Mr Norman, the Aylesbury printer. The world had moved a long way from the old wooden double-pull press when this picture of the printing works was taken on 18 December 1964. The building was demolished in 1966 for the access road to the multi-storey car-park. Nowadays printing is done out of town by specialists and the days of 'stop press' news are over.

'One corner – the prettiest and most popular – at the new telephone exchange in New Street. They are all set for the big change over to automatic dial system. Automation won't drive the girls away though. They will be needed for trunk calls and inquiries. And you'd be surprised how many of those there are each day.' *Bucks Advertiser*, March 1957.

Those were the days when postmen earned £11 15s a week. These two young Aylesbury postmen, Andrew Ferris (left) and Graham Brown, took telegrams on these BSA Bantams. In their spare time they took part in the 1964 Motor Cyclist of the Year competition. Aylesbury's first post office opened in 1685 and it took a week to deliver a letter to London.

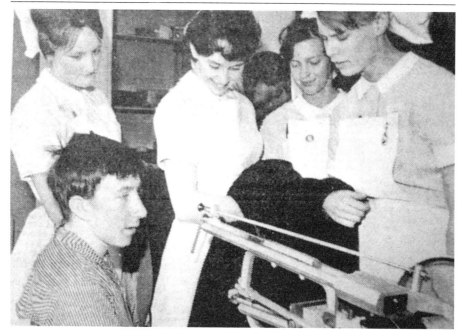

Stoke Mandeville Hospital was founded during the Second World War to treat horrific burns. Early this century Ralph Rayner, who was suffering from scarlet fever, remembers being taken from his home in a closed cart and being shut in Stoke Mandeville Isolation Hospital for six weeks without visitors. This picture shows a motor-cycle crash victim receiving occupational therapy at the spinal injuries unit, 1966.

The Great Train Robbers are seen here leaving Aylesbury Court in 1964. The *Bucks Advertiser* reported: 'Through the small windows the guilty took their last look at Aylesbury, the town where their fate was decided.' The van's number seems most appropriate!

Ware's slaughterhouse, Buckingham Street, just before its demolition in 1964. Ivatt's shoe business is on the far right and the Eagle pub is on the left.

Former Whitchurch policeman Les Fowler driving one of his lorries, late 1960s. His business grew as a result of his friendship with local haulier Sid Goss. In the early days Les remembers delivering baked beans to Sid Macey's shop in Bicester Road: 'I used to wake him up in the morning, never took my finger off the bell till he answered.' The Gatehouse-based firm is now part of the Dentressangle group.

Section Five

TROUBLED TIMES

Members of Wendover Fire Brigade attend to a car

crash outside The Swan at Wendover, 1971.

The first Remembrance Day parade to the Market Square Memorial, 1920. Contrary to popular myths, most men do not enjoy violence any more than most women. But when Kitchener's finger pointed at a young man in 1914, he either went or faced mockery from women ready to give him a white feather to mark his cowardice. War is a dirty business and men who have never experienced it might seem a little over-enthusiastic, as we see on page 76. The fact is that a most common sound on the First World War battlefields was that of young men calling out for their mothers as they died. But propaganda paints a different picture. When the boys came back to Aylesbury they expected 'homes fit for heroes', as the government had promised. They got some in Southcourt – but they did not get much peace. Unemployment was not so bad around Aylesbury, but there was hardship and plenty of tramps looking for hope. A decade later there was another 'great war' and even bigger upheaval in Aylesbury's fortunes. Like most places, Aylesbury has had its fair share of troubles, but the postwar period was meant to be an age of unparalleled prosperity, with the Welfare State guaranteeing good education and health care for all. Fire, police and ambulance services improved when they became county run, in 1948. It would soon be a case of 'you've never had it so good'. So why have there been so many troubled times?

The first Remembrance Day parade through Kingsbury Square after the First World War. 'Aeroplanes repaired' was painted on the roof of The Aylesbury Motor Co. building (left).

Young soldiers go laughing off to war. This is a section from the unbroken columns that marched through town in September 1914.

This tank is being driven to Kingsbury Square, 1920. There it replaced a galvanised public lavatory and served as an unusual war memorial for nine years. Small boys managed to get inside it and continued to use it as a public lavatory until it was cut up. The cutting torch ignited petrol left in the tank, causing an explosion, which damaged buildings.

Primrose Miller selling poppies just before Aylesbury's first 'Great War' Remembrance Day.

This picture shows one of Alan Cobham's flying-circus aircraft on a field near the site of Adams' Garage in Tring Road. The First World War stimulated air travel and leisure, and turned de Rothschild's Halton Estate into an army camp, and later a famous RAF base. Confidence in air travel grew. But in 1934 tragedy struck when Cobham's Handley Page, the 'Youth of New Zealand', crashed at College Farm, Aston Clinton, killing four crew members.

This is Coombe Hill Monument, to the men who died in the Boer War. Standing 852 ft above sea level, it is not surprising that lightning struck it twice. This view shows damage after the first hit on 29 January 1938. Reporter John How wrote: 'The sky was purple, the lightning terrific when at 2 a.m. a heavy flash hit the monument. The 64 ft column was struck down to within a few feet of its base.'

Fire Officer Norris with one of the brigade's modern Dennis fire engines, 1920s. This was a great improvement over the days when firemen needed to be knocked up and had to catch their horses. Aylesbury's superior equipment and training was crucial to getting control over the 'Great Fire of Winslow High Street' on 13 December 1933. Spectator Reg Langley said: 'If Aylesbury hadn't got there it would have been a lot worse. They immediately decided to tackle it from the back and away from the direction of the wind.' Aylesbury has had years of experience of big fires. The biggest was in 1750; it started near the site of the now-demolished St John's Church in Cambridge Street, and was caused by the accidental lighting of furze heaps collected for brick making at Lee's kiln. Within three hours twenty-six houses had been destroyed, including Lee's, and the Dog and Duck pub.

The Great Fire of Winslow High Street reputedly started when a boy dumped hot ashes from cooking next to a dry wooden fence, which was next to a builder's yard. It was a windy night and former Aylesbury footballer Reg Langley's mum woke him when she saw the glow in the sky.

There was no county fire brigade in the 1920s. Unless the fire was exceptional, parishes looked after their own. This conflagration was caused by youngsters who purchased fireworks from this Granborough shop and accidentally set fire to it.

A child ran out into the road and driver Reg Baldwin, on the Red Rover route from Aylesbury, had no chance of avoiding a fatal collision, summer 1933.

A crowd of local children watched this LCS milk tanker run down the long hill south of Winslow en route to Aylesbury in 1934. They knew it would crash when it reached the tiny humpback bridge over Shipton Brook. The County Council took over responsibility for highways in 1931 and were preparing bypasses countywide to cope with increasing traffic demands – and to prevent more accidents like this one.

Civil Defence volunteers, Aylesbury, 1941.

Women's Voluntary Service members in Market Square during a march past for Winston Churchill's wartime visit.

Ron Rayner's converted ex-US Army Diamond T lorry at work rescuing the rescuers. This Aylesbury fire engine skidded on wintry roads in the early 1970s. Craftsman Ron, who built his own breakdown equipment, had the contract to repair all the county's fire engines and had this one back on the road before the end of the day.

Ron Rayner stands – very much king of his castle – on the side of an overturned trailer loaded with coffin wood. The accident happened at the notoriously sharp Hartwell corner near the Bugle Horn pub in 1972.

This tanker crashed on the A413 just north of Winslow, at Easter 1966. Aylesbury Brigade took charge of the fire-fighting and Ron Rayner took charge of the debris. Winslow girls Margaret and Sue Langley were first on the scene. Looking along the ditch they could see the driver had got through his cab window and they managed to pull him clear.

A fire at Hartwell House, 1963. The house had been sold to Ernest Cook, grandson of Sir Thomas, in 1938. The war prevented him from occupying it and instead Canadian troops were stationed there. When they left, Cook didn't want it and looked for suitable tenants who would put the house to good use.

The House of Citizenship, a girls' finishing school, took the lease until 1983. Here we see firemen extinguishing the 1963 fire, which destroyed the roof; water damaged the first floor.

The Hartwell House fire is nearly out and this Aylesbury fireman takes a well-earned rest among some rescued furniture and fittings.

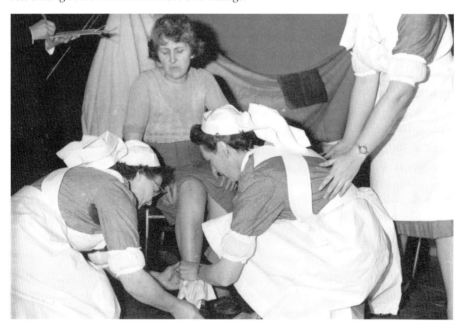

Pat Otway acts as a patient at a first-aid competition for the St John Ambulance Brigade at Quarrendon School, 1959. Pat recalls that the blood was very realistic. Her husband Jack joined the ambulance service when it was voluntary and continued when the County Council took it over. The emergency services have come a long way since this picture was taken but they still have need for constant practice and dedication; there will always be troubles to test them.

TAKING IT EASY

Possibly a member of the Lee family ready for the

freedom of the open roads from Hartwell House,

1890s.

An Edwardian bank holiday sports day at Hazell's grounds (which became Vale Park in 1929). Those were the days of simple pleasures. Ralph Rayner observed: 'Folk didn't talk of what came naturally, they just got on with it. That was why there were such big families.' Nowadays television pundits interpret life's meanings for the average person and life seems much more complicated, even while we play. But, for all the new-fangled ways of 1959, there were still some pretty basic instincts at work when this *Bucks Advertiser* report was made about women watching wrestling at Aylesbury's Grosvenor Rooms. The reporter spoke to Mrs Jones, who was with her daughter. She explained: 'I think it's a relief to see other people let off steam in these days when we are all so civilised.' Mrs Radwell, who had been shouting advice to the underdog, said: 'We used to watch wrestling on television and that's how we got interested.' Miss Phillipa Good, aged 17, explained: 'It's much more entertaining than the cinema.'

William Stanley's daughter, Louise Emily, and son, Charles Jabez, with two of their father's splendid products from the Walton Cycle & Motor Works, 1910. Cycling was much safer for children in those days even if the machines were cumbersome.

Baptist preacher Benjamin Keach in Aylesbury stocks, after his trial in October 1664. He was found guilty of producing a pamphlet against child baptism and other church conventions, and was placed in the pillory to 'rivet the gaze of the rabble upon him and to expose him helplessly to their derision, kicks and cuffs' (Robert Gibbs, *A History of Aylesbury*). His discomfiture must have provided a lot of pleasure to those who did not enjoy or know how to think!

Maypole dancing at Hartwell House, 1897.

Some traditions survive. Aylesbury runners are among competitors in this 1970 County Cross Country Championship at Waddesdon Manor. The author, Robert Cook, is Wolverton runner no. 45 (third from right). He came second in the junior class. Pat Ferguson is no. 83 (second left); he represented Aylesbury Vale AC.

Aylesbury United Football Club early this century, when Dark Lantern pub landlord Frederick Silver Haydon was chairman. The players are: Tom Keen (goalkeeper), Frederick Silver Haydon, Horace Dixon, Joseph J. Thorpe, Will Marsh, Fred Gilbert, Jack Scott, Albert Cherry, Charlie Stevens, Bob Osborne, Ernie Sear, Aran Ellis, Jack Woodford, Bill Smith, Bill Brown, Percy North, Bill Rogers.

Aylesbury Junior Football Club early this century. War would soon disrupt their simple pleasures.

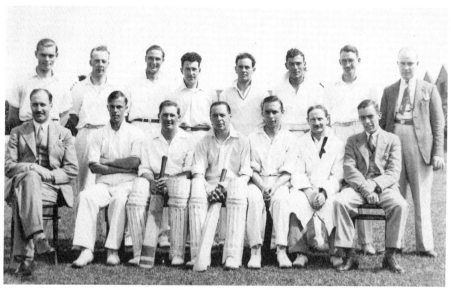

Between the wars, this Bifurcated Tubular Rivet cricket team was one of the best. Leslie 'Dick' Goodchild (far right) was the score-keeper.

The slumbering iron lion seen here to the left was one of a pair presented to the town by Baron Ferdinand de Rothschild in 1888. Goodridge's dining rooms are on the right, and gas lighting is in place. The struggle for lighting began in 1800, when Colonel Brown opened a subscription for 'a few miserably dull oil lamps' (Gibbs). The town was lit by, and could cook with, gas in 1834. An electricity scheme began in 1915.

A Sunday School treat in Aylesbury Vale, 1908.

This group includes Ted Miller (who ran Aylesbury Steam laundry), his wife Primrose, her sister Rose and Rose's husband Fred Goodchild. They are pictured at Egyptian Springs, Hartwell, in the 1920s. When they were children Primrose and Rose used to help their father at the brickworks, nearby in Hartwell.

Off for a spin through Southcourt into the country lanes, 1926. Aylesbury's pioneering motorists did not worry about seat belts or driving tests.

Coombe Hill Monument is not the highest point in the Chilterns, but was an ideal resting-place for these weary walkers to stop and enjoy the view over the vale, 1920s.

Carnival time, 1935. The lorry for this float was provided by local hauliers Sulston's.

A carnival scene in Exchange Street, July 1973. The fashions have changed and the clothes look more dated, in our fashion-crazy times, than those of the 1935 carnival. The approaching float lorry belonged to the Gatehouse-based Doughnut Corporation of America – one of the first companies established on the new industrial estate in the early sixties.

Driving and stoking this pre-First World War Foden steam wagon was thirsty work – just as well Aylesbury had so many pubs to cool a man down. The Falcon and Greyhound were demolished for 1960s' road improvements in an age of more and faster traffic. The Aylesbury Brewery Company, which owned both pubs, took over the Walton Brewery Company in 1895.

The King's Head, Market Square, 1930s. This fine Tudor inn is now preserved by the National Trust, but sadly is rather concealed by recent town-centre developments.

The old Borough Arms, 19 June 1959. This was rebuilt during the town's 1960s face-lift.

The old Hen and Chickens, 14 February 1965. It was photographed just before its demolition to make way for the ring road which obliterated the old Oxford Road–Whitehill junction. The turnpike collector's house stood by this junction, alongside the Seven Stars beerhouse. Those were the prewar days, when 'Ducky' Weston used to lead his ducks from Mount Street to water at Bearbrook.

The seventeenth-century Rising Sun was once a welcome sight for weary travellers coming off the dusty Oxford Road and into town via the steep and narrow hill of Castle Street. By 1964, when this picture was taken, the sun had set. The advancing ring road required its demolition.

Hazell's works band, 1938. The bandmaster is Jack Alderson.

The Vale Open-Air Swimming-Pool was the venue of the swimming galas in carnival week, summer 1935.

Bifurcated Tubular Rivets children's Christmas party, late 1940s. Many old local employers followed this paternalistic tradition.

Simon Vincent Robinson and wife Alice Ellen at their home, Mobberley, in Wendover Road, early 1960s. This picture was taken during a party to celebrate Mr Robinson's 75th birthday. The name of Marks, the major local supplier of marquees, is visible on the canvas in the background.

Folk dancing at Aylesbury Grammar School Country Fair, 1929. This school was gutted by fire in 1953, the year of its 354th anniversary.

Talbot Rothwell's comedy *Queen Elizabeth Slept Here*, staged by Aylesbury Dramatic Society at Hazell's, 27 November 1953. Tickets cost 5s, and the *Bucks Advertiser* praised 17-year-old Shirley Duff: 'As is customary with novices, she was given the part of a maid. While maintaining the slovenly demeanour demanded of the part, Shirley kept her head high and clearly enunciated each word.'

'Sailor Girls' dance a hornpipe for the boys of Aylesbury Methodist Youth Club at their 1965 dinner. Modern times obviously had their good points!

· Margaret Neale produced this Aylesbury College drama, *Ring Round the Moon*, in 1969. The cast included staff and students. Margaret succeeded Annie Castledine, who is currently working with the National Theatre. The college cost £315,000 and was opened in 1964 by Princess Alexandra. Its first drama production was Charlotte Hastings' *Bonaventure*, about youth and rebellion.

This 1929 picture shows that pop music is no new thing. Lyn Corson (right) from the USA is jamming in an Aylesbury back garden with his 'Uncle' Bill Whitlock, whom he was visiting.

These Aylesbury youngsters are well aware of the town's pop music tradition. It's the age of the original mods and they are getting their act together in a Victoria Street backyard, 1962. From left to right: Maurice Dell, Peter Adams, Gary Saunders, Michael Marks.

St John Ambulance members lead a parade along the High Street, June 1959. The Granada Cinema (left) was still in its heyday, but was facing fierce competition from the plusher Odeon, which opened in June 1937. Boris Karloff no doubt helped to pull the crowds!

Lady Baden-Powell meeting Aylesbury's Girl Guides, 1966.

Nubar Gulbenkian enjoying Whaddon's point-to-point horse-races, 1964. He was a distinctive figure in the Aylesbury district, especially on his horse. He wrote about his fascinating life in *Pantaxia*, in which he described one of his interests as 'keeping people on their toes'.

Ron Rayner and his volunteers pose by a carnival float which warns of the dangers of taking life too easy, 1972. Seven years earlier, the *Bucks Advertiser* had reported 'Misery and Grief' on the county's roads, with 100 killed and 4,286 injured.

A young Princess Diana arrives on the Grange School sports field on her way to open the new Hale Leys shopping centre, February 1983.

An old cattle market close to extinction. Here, it stands behind a new Civic Centre and Reg Maxwell Swimming-Pool, built for an Aylesbury population who might want to take it easy. This picture was taken on the last market day in 1987. Vale farmers, backed by EC subsidies, have shifted towards arable. Winslow is now the only surviving cattle market in Bucks.

TIMES WERE
A' CHANGING

Away with the old, c. 1964.

Of these five views, dating from the 1950s, only the bottom right has changed much. The Bull's Head was popular with businessmen, farmers and reporters such as *Bucks Advertiser* editor John How. Inside was a merry hum of the old Bucks accents. The false front put the finishing touches on this show of old England, but it was actually the idea of its more European proprietor, G. Gargini. He was also the owner of the original Market Theatre, and was mayor in the 1930s. The Bull's Head was demolished in 1969 and the site is now the entrance to Hale Leys shopping centre. The old County Hall (top left) is now home to the County Court; it was gutted by fire in the late 1960s. The Corn Exchange stood to its right, where the original White Hart had stood from 1814 to 1864. It seems that Aylesbury has been forever changing but has always seemed quaint.

Market Square, late 1890s. The Clock Tower was built with proceeds from the sale of the rubble of Market House (demolished in 1866) and public subscriptions. It cost £882 and opened in July 1876. The sale of livestock in the square ceased in 1927. The new market was just beyond the archway under the Corn Exchange (left), and vehicle access was from the other side of the block, via Exchange Street. The clock has survived many changes but is now largely symbolic. Technology measures time by other means and seems to speed it up! At 12 noon on 7 March 1957 Aylesbury Mayor Glyn Davies switched on the New Street automatic telephone exchange. The ceremonial gathering then heard TIM, the speaking-clock. Times had changed, as the famous 1960s protest singer Bob Dylan had often pointed out. There would soon be plenty more protest in Aylesbury as more than time changed, and a whole generation of Aylesbury's youth moved 'beyond their parents' command'. Meanwhile, what kind of example were the redevelopers setting for rising generations? Solicitor Alan Jones, representing two of the objectors, said: 'Aylesbury Borough Council's scheme will wipe out a lot of traders who have spent a lifetime building up their businesses.'

The north side of Market Square, 1920s. Barbara Thorpe fondly remembers this old Market Square for its fairs, with sideshows and stalls selling home-made toffee: '[the toffee seller] stretched it and flung it about before he sold it. There were no worries about food hygiene in those days.' The George was demolished to make way for Burton's in 1936.

During the 1930s livestock haulier J. Goss' lorry carried animals from Westcott, a few miles west of Aylesbury, to the market. Westcott was famous for its Rocket Propulsion Establishment, which was an intended target for the IRA in the 1970s.

A busy Market Square, 1890s. On 18 March 1893 the *Bucks Herald* warned of sheep scab: 'Cases of this malady are reported on the premises of Mr Thomas Rutland, Boughton Paton and Mr John King, Quarrendon.'

A quiet scene on Berryfields Farm, near Quarrendon, mid-1950s. Note the healthy array of wild flowers at the roadside.

The new livestock market expanded rapidly on to former park land adjacent to Exchange Street. Local pubs and inns became busiest on Wednesdays and Saturdays, and the smithy at the back of The Bear was kept busy all day. Reg Jellis of Cheddington, who carried livestock to Aylesbury in the market's 1950s heyday, said: 'Folk brought store cattle off the hills for fattening in the Vale. I've been out at midnight working. Didn't worry about the hours them days. Just kept on going till you was done. Aylesbury took fatstock Wednesday, dairy animals Saturday. There was a bit of a fight as to who would sell first. C.A. Rogers started as Reader's auctioneer before the war.'

C.A. Rogers attends to a sheep auction at Aylesbury market, late 1930s.

The corner shop, Great Western Street. Railway passengers bought morning papers and sweets here en route to the station and the London train. George Rayner's, one of the shops on the right, used to hang rabbits up outside its butcher's shop. Colin Harvey-Taylor comments: 'I loved their splendid array of turkeys at Christmas, when I was a boy.'

In 1955 the pupils and staff of Queen's Park School moved to Grange School, which was then a very modern complex. The queen (seen here) paid a visit shortly after it opened. There had been much competition to occupy the premises, not least from the grammar school, and Queen's Park School made speedy moves to ensure that no other schools laid claim to them. Now in its 40th anniversary year, the school has had four headteachers and continues to be in the forefront of local education. The old Queen's Park still exists as a resource and support centre.

Adams' Garage, Tring Road, just after the Second World War. This family business was established in 1943. Visible here are the original three petrol pumps and one dummy. The old buildings, and Coffee Lane (left), disappeared when the relief road was built in 1962.

R.P. Richards and Son's timber yard is visible in the background of this mid-1950s scene at Aylesbury market. By this time the market was equipped with iron animal pens instead of the earlier wooden 'hurdles'.

Aylesbury cattle-lorry drivers, 1955. Reg Jellis (far right) said: 'If you drove a cattle lorry in them days, you had brown boots and turned your trousers up.'

Market day, 1966. The new County Office building, nicknamed 'Fred's Folly', looms up over the old ones. The building was designed by County Architect Fred Pooley and is seen here near completion. A Marriott's builder's sign is visible at the top of the building.

A GIANT ON THE ROADS

Livestock was still big business in the Vale at the end of the 1960s. Grosmith's, animal feed producers based on the old Haddenham wartime airfield, reckoned it would need lorries as big as the one shown here to deliver its goods to farmers. At 32 tons the lorry seems small by today's standards.

Here is a bit of organic vegetable growing in one of Southcourt's large back gardens, *c.* 1967. Space was not at so much of a premium in the 1920s and the development contrasts with the more recent Walton Court. John Reed recalls the early days when Southcourt had its white- and blue-collar areas. By April 1965 the estate was so affluent with motor cars that United Counties discontinued the through bus service.

Southcourt replaced a lot of condemned houses such as these ones photographed in the King's Head yard, 12 August 1958. Housing demand was considerable. Wartime newcomers moved into the emergency Molefield Estate, near today's King Edward Avenue, and the influx has continued ever since.

Not only the buildings were changing. In May 1965 these high-school girls were given the headmistress's permission 'to slip into blouses and skirts and summer dresses' designed by her. Sixth formers were allowed to wear 'anything within reason'. Pupil Angela Ravens said: 'This will be good training for college.'

While the chief constable was fending off criticism that crime was rising in surrounding villages, WP Sergeant Sonia Hackett was just back from 'a week of wonderful hospitality in Amsterdam', where she was 'often mobbed' and had to sign autographs. Here she is modelling her new summer uniform, 1965.

Looking south over Aylesbury High Street, 1959. Hazell's chimney stands on the horizon, to the left. It was demolished in the 1970s to make way for the Wyn Jones Centre. Just out of view to the left, the 120 ft chimney of the Nestles condensed milk factory stood as a monument to another revolution. It was built in 1870 by the Aylesbury Condensed Milk Company, which boiled locally produced milk down to half its bulk, and added carbonate of soda. The finished product was shipped to London via the Cheddington railway link. Strangely, the redundant chimney survived until June 1994, but a lot of other old landmarks have not. This scene shows many new shop fronts, but behind them was little room for business to expand, and traffic was becoming a problem. Space was needed and so the Silver Street area was chosen for demolition. Alan Jones, solicitor for the objectors, said: 'Since 1955 the Borough Council had pursued a creeping *fait accompli* technique by buying up property in the area.' He added that one of his clients, George T. Rayner, the Great Western Street butcher, had traded for twenty-six years, playing his part in the community and investing his life savings in the business, and was therefore entitled to 'fair treatment'. (Francis Frith Collection)

Aylesbury High Street on a summer's day in 1959. This view is looking north-west from Exchange Street. The Chandos Hotel was named after Lord Chandos of Buckingham and was demolished in the early 1970s to make way for an office block. (Francis Frith Collection)

This Upper Hundreds site was one of the best examples of Aylesbury's 1960s' decay and was an inspiration to those who wanted change. Today the 1990s' inner relief road passes this way.

The rear of Silver Street, near the site of the old Falcon public house, 28 August 1964.

Silver Lane, 14 August 1964,

Lower Silver Street just before its demolition, 8 August 1964.

The same scene two months later.

The top of Silver Street, showing the Dark Lantern pub (with the bay windows, centre right), 1964. This is one of the oldest buildings in an area comprising mainly sixteenth- and seventeenth-century dwellings. The old pub survived, becoming a haunt of youth in the 'swinging sixties and 'spaced out seventies' (D.J. Huntley)

Going, going . . . and it will soon all be gone. The top of Silver Street during its demolition, October 1964. (D.J. Huntley)

The junction of Silver Street and Market Square. The 'last day of sale' sign attached to the right-hand shop front warns that these are the final moments of an old town centre.

A rare view of Market Square, looking north-east. Twenty-six separate properties were to be demolished in the redevelopment zone. There were seventeen objectors, including Mary Lord's Stage School. Out of this destruction arose the concrete shops and walkways of Friar's Square; this was so barren, thought some, that it was not surprising Stanley Kubrick chose to film the violent and destructive *Clockwork Orange* there.

A modern Red Rover bus leaves the new concrete Friar's development, which incorporated a purpose-built bus station, thus relieving congestion on Kingsbury.

Looking north from the Royal Bucks Hospital in March 1988, during its final days as a specialist maternity unit. In the distance is the trendy new Watermead development and the dry ski slope: both of these say much about the new face of Aylesbury.

Acknowledgements

This is the most difficult part of the book for me to write because it is impossible for me to measure the help that I have been given by so many kind people. I hope this book does justice to what they have given me in time, memories and photographs. Some of them are quoted in the book; others, such as Bob and Gill Dickins, have guided me. Luckily, John Reed recorded the crucial period before and during the 1960s demolition and has shared some of his work here. Reg Jellis has provided the pictures of the rise and fall of the farmers' market. I feel guilty not saying more of everyone else's contribution, which has been immeasurable. There have been so many directly involved in helping me, I can only complete my thanks in the form of an alphabetical list:

S. Bensalah • M. Blane • L. Brazier • *Bucks Herald* • D. Carter
S. Collier • Jane Culler and Julian Hunt, of the County Library
R. and G. Dickins • Historic Hotels • T. Foley • David Fowler
Mr and Mrs L. Fowler • Francis Frith Collection • W. Garner
Dick Goodchild • T. Goodwin • Colin Harvey-Taylor • R. Hills • John How
Ann Hughes • D.J. Huntley • Reg Jellis • M. Langley • M. Leather • D.J. Lee
Olive Martin • Andrew Miller • Primrose Miller • Irene Mortimer
the late Norman Newman • John Otway • Margaret Otway
Judy Ounsworth • Mrs P. Phillips • Mr and Mrs Ralph Rayner • Ron Rayner
T. Redman • A.J. Reed • John Robinson • L.H.C. Rogers • C. Seabright
J. Skinner • Barbara Thorpe • Mr and Mrs F. Taylor • Una Taylor
Jonathon Thompson • P. Ward

Finally, thanks to my wife, Nicola, whose help and advice is always very important to me.

BRITAIN IN OLD PHOTOGRAPHS

To order any of these titles please telephone Littlehampton Book Services on 01903 721596

ALDERNEY

Alderney: A Second Selection, *B Bonnard*

BEDFORDSHIRE

Bedfordshire at Work, *N Lutt*

BERKSHIRE

Maidenhead, *M Hayles & D Hedges*
Around Maidenhead, *M Hayles & B Hedges*
Reading, *P Southerton*
Reading: A Second Selection, *P Southerton*
Sandhurst and Crowthorne, *K Dancy*
Around Slough, *J Hunter & K Hunter*
Around Thatcham, *P Allen*
Around Windsor, *B Hedges*

BUCKINGHAMSHIRE

Buckingham and District, *R Cook*
High Wycombe, *R Goodearl*
Around Stony Stratford, *A Lambert*

CHESHIRE

Cheshire Railways, *M Hitches*
Chester, *S Nichols*

CLWYD

Clwyd Railways, *M Hitches*

CLYDESDALE

Clydesdale, *Lesmahagow Parish Historical Association*

CORNWALL

Cornish Coast, *T Bowden*
Falmouth, *P Gilson*
Lower Fal, *P Gilson*
Around Padstow, *M McCarthy*
Around Penzance, *J Holmes*
Penzance and Newlyn, *J Holmes*
Around Truro, *A Lyne*
Upper Fal, *P Gilson*

CUMBERLAND

Cockermouth and District, *J Bernard Bradbury*
Keswick and the Central Lakes, *J Marsh*
Around Penrith, *F Boyd*
Around Whitehaven, *H Fancy*

DERBYSHIRE

Derby, *D Buxton*
Around Matlock, *D Barton*

DEVON

Colyton and Seaton, *T Gosling*
Dawlish and Teignmouth, *G Gosling*
Devon Aerodromes, *K Saunders*
Exeter, *P Thomas*
Exmouth and Budleigh Salterton, *T Gosling*
From Haldon to Mid-Dartmoor, *T Hall*
Honiton and the Otter Valley, *J Yallop*
Around Kingsbridge, *K Tanner*
Around Seaton and Sidmouth, *T Gosling*
Seaton, Axminster and Lyme Regis, *T Gosling*

DORSET

Around Blandford Forum, *B Cox*
Bournemouth, *M Colman*
Bridport and the Bride Valley, *J Burrell & S Humphries*
Dorchester, *T Gosling*
Around Gillingham, *P Crocker*

DURHAM

Darlington, *G Flynn*
Darlington: A Second Selection, *G Flynn*
Durham People, *M Richardson*
Houghton-le-Spring and Hetton-le-Hole, *K Richardson*
Houghton-le-Spring and Hetton-le-Hole:
 A Second Selection, *K Richardson*
Sunderland, *S Miller & B Bell*
Teesdale, *D Coggins*
Teesdale: A Second Selection, *P Raine*
Weardale, *J Crosby*
Weardale: A Second Selection, *J Crosby*

DYFED

Aberystwyth and North Ceredigion,
 Dyfed Cultural Services Dept
Haverfordwest, *Dyfed Cultural Services Dept*
Upper Tywi Valley, *Dyfed Cultural Services Dept*

ESSEX

Around Grays, *B Evans*

GLOUCESTERSHIRE

Along the Avon from Stratford to Tewkesbury, *J Jeremiah*
Cheltenham: A Second Selection, *R Whiting*
Cheltenham at War, *P Gill*
Cirencester, *J Welsford*
Around Cirencester, *E Cuss & P Griffiths*
Forest, The, *D Mullin*
Gloucester, *J Voyce*
Around Gloucester, *A Sutton*
Gloucester: From the Walwin Collection, *J Voyce*
North Cotswolds, *D Viner*
Severn Vale, *A Sutton*
Stonehouse to Painswick, *A Sutton*
Stroud and the Five Valleys, *S Gardiner & L Padin*
Stroud and the Five Valleys: A Second Selection,
 S Gardiner & L Padin
Stroud's Golden Valley, *S Gardiner & L Padin*
Stroudwater and Thames & Severn Canals,
 E Cuss & S Gardiner
Stroudwater and Thames & Severn Canals: A Second
 Selection, *E Cuss & S Gardiner*
Tewkesbury and the Vale of Gloucester, *C Hilton*
Thornbury to Berkeley, *J Hudson*
Uley, Dursley and Cam, *A Sutton*
Wotton-under-Edge to Chipping Sodbury, *A Sutton*

GWYNEDD

Anglesey, *M Hitches*
Gwynedd Railways, *M Hitches*
Around Llandudno, *M Hitches*
Vale of Conwy, *M Hitches*

HAMPSHIRE

Gosport, *J Sadden*
Portsmouth, *P Rogers & D Francis*

HEREFORDSHIRE

Herefordshire, *A Sandford*

HERTFORDSHIRE

Barnet, *I Norrie*
Hitchin, *A Fleck*
St Albans, *S Mullins*
Stevenage, *M Appleton*

ISLE OF MAN

The Tourist Trophy, *B Snelling*

ISLE OF WIGHT

Newport, *D Parr*
Around Ryde, *D Parr*

JERSEY

Jersey: A Third Selection, *R Lemprière*

KENT

Bexley, *M Scott*
Broadstairs and St Peter's, *J Whyman*
Bromley, Keston and Hayes, *M Scott*
Canterbury: A Second Selection, *D Butler*
Chatham and Gillingham, *P MacDougall*
Chatham Dockyard, *P MacDougall*
Deal, *J Broady*
Early Broadstairs and St Peter's, *B Wootton*
East Kent at War, *D Collyer*
Eltham, *J Kennett*
Folkestone: A Second Selection, *A Taylor & E Rooney*
Goudhurst to Tenterden, *A Guilmant*
Gravesend, *R Hiscock*
Around Gravesham, *R Hiscock & D Grierson*
Herne Bay, *J Hawkins*
Lympne Airport, *D Collyer*
Maidstone, *I Hales*
Margate, *R Clements*
RAF Hawkinge, *R Humphreys*
RAF Manston, *RAF Manston History Club*
RAF Manston: A Second Selection,
 RAF Manston History Club
Ramsgate and Thanet Life, *D Perkins*
Romney Marsh, *E Carpenter*
Sandwich, *C Wanostrocht*
Around Tonbridge, *C Bell*
Tunbridge Wells, *M Rowlands & I Beavis*
Tunbridge Wells: A Second Selection,
 M Rowlands & I Beavis
Around Whitstable, *C Court*
Wingham, Adisham and Littlebourne, *M Crane*

LANCASHIRE

Around Barrow-in-Furness, *J Garbutt & J Marsh*
Blackpool, *C Rothwell*
Bury, *J Hudson*
Chorley and District, *J Smith*
Fleetwood, *C Rothwell*
Heywood, *J Hudson*
Around Kirkham, *C Rothwell*
Lancashire North of the Sands, *J Garbutt & J Marsh*
Around Lancaster, *S Ashworth*
Lytham St Anne's, *C Rothwell*
North Fylde, *C Rothwell*
Radcliffe, *J Hudson*
Rossendale, *B Moore & N Dunnachie*

LEICESTERSHIRE

Around Ashby-de-la-Zouch, *K Hillier*
Charnwood Forest, *I Keil, W Humphrey & D Wix*
Leicester, *D Burton*
Leicester: A Second Selection, *D Burton*
Melton Mowbray, *T Hickman*
Around Melton Mowbray, *T Hickman*
River Soar, *D Wix, P Shacklock & I Keil*
Rutland, *T Clough*
Vale of Belvoir, *T Hickman*
Around the Welland Valley, *S Mastoris*

LINCOLNSHIRE

Grimsby, *J Tierney*
Around Grimsby, *J Tierney*
Grimsby Docks, *J Tierney*
Lincoln, *D Cuppleditch* Scunthorpe, *D Taylor*